Gestalt Practice Metaphysics

The Gestalt Legacy Project

Gestalt Practice Metaphysics

Copyright © 2014 *Día de Muertos*
by John F. Callahan
for The Gestalt Legacy Project

ISBN: 978-1-312-53970-9

"Trust process, support process,
and get out of the way."
--Richard Price

Mind is a metaphysical field of information.

Gestalt is the configuration of ontology.

The process of life is congregational.

The pattern of awareness survives.

Practice is transformational.

Mind is a field of information[1] that supports the configuration of embodied life and the formation of the human self properly understood as the regulatory process of cognition, emotion, behavior and relationship.

The field of mind is metaphysical in the sense that it is not accessible to measurement by techniques currently known to human beings. This failure does not compromise the existence of the field, but merely suggests the primitive nature of human epistemology. Nor is the field inaccessible to human consciousness. For this reason the field may be more appropriately described as a phenomenological field of mind.

---

[1] Field in this context means a condition that extends throughout space with varying degrees of influence depending upon location and receptor, like the force of an electric field on an electron or proton.

The origin of the field of mind can be traced to an era estimated to be about 380,000 years after the so-called Big Bang.[2] The Big Bang can be characterized as a singularity. There was no "beginning" of the Universe. Beginning implies duration and location, and the source of the singularity is indeterminate - a state equivalent to the eternal and omnipresent. And there could be no "nothing" before the singularity, because absolute nothingness is an inherently false concept. The only accurate way to think about a state prefiguring the Universe is to conceive of potentiality without form.

_____

[2] Big Bang is a terrible name for the singularity, first used by Fred Hoyle on a television program in 1949, and later propagated because of the public appeal of its dramatic but inaccurate connotation.

Except for miniscule irregularities in space remaining from the brief inflationary era, the Universe was a homogeneous plasma, until photons decoupled from matter. This happened about 380,000 years after the singularity, when temperature fell below 4000 degrees Kelvin. Photon release was the beginning of information, in the sense of a discernible difference. At the same time, mind emerged as a phenomenological field of information.

The origin of information began with an emergence, both of what is knowable as the physical world of large-scale structure and as the phenomenological world of mind. The Newtonian/Einsteinian world of matter in space-time emerged from the underlying quantum world. Simultaneously, what has been described as the world of Geist emerged from the unknowable as a corresponding phenomenal field of mind.

Life is an organized, coherent, localized decrease in entropy, synonymous with being. Living entities are coherent configurations of matter and energy organized by information. The level of organization describes the decrease in entropy.

The phenomenon of life is much more general than we are inclined to believe. There are many more living entities than we care to know about. A planet may be alive. The Earth, for instance, is a living being. A cluster of galaxies may be alive. Just because we can't imagine the nature of their lives does not mean they are not living. Life happens; so it may be possible to think of a fundamental principle, an *élan vital*, as the creator. But it is just as easy to think of life as an emergent organizational feature of the Universe, in which entropy is locally decreased by a coherent configuration of energy processing mediated by information.

The patterns of life exist as information in the field of mind.

Localized organizational patterns of the field, which already have been partially described as morphogenetic fields, support the predominant organization of living processes. Thus the field of mind is both embodied and transcendent.

Life may be embodied in a wide variety of forms across a broad range, from bacteria and what is colloquially recognized as "the body," to planetary objects and groups of galaxies. The identifying feature of life is a coherent localized decrease in entropy. The phenomenological feature is awareness. Awareness is an emergent phenomenon that is crucial to the maintenance of living embodiment, as well as the establishment of fundamental presence in the field.

Awareness is an emergent characteristic of life that does not require human consciousness. Homeostasis requires awareness. All living systems must have an appropriate form of awareness. Life must maintain contact with its environment in order to process the energy relevant to its continued existence. Among the many narcissistic ideas of humankind is that consciousness is some kind of unique process. Human consciousness is a function of awareness. And awareness is actually a feature of any coherent, self-regulating system, like the Earth. So it is possible to imagine, and perhaps even experience, forms of awareness that are different from human consciousness; and it is egotistical to believe that other forms of being, which transcend human being, do not exist. But transcendent beings are companions, not creators.

Humans have the capacity to transform their awareness and change the character of their being.

Awareness is an experience that is available to all beings. But it is possible to block awareness, to become more like matter than process. Awareness can be narrowed or expanded. Since awareness is common to all life, it can be a shared experience. So humans have the ability to both increase and reorient their awareness.

Transformation of human awareness can be facilitated by experimentation and practice.

Humans have the capacity to assist other beings in the project of transforming their awareness. This ability goes beyond the evolutionary strategy of community. Humans have the capacity to promote awareness in others, even with the objective of liberating others from the suffering inherent in the human condition. Qualities of empathy and compassion, which are characteristic of this ability, are talents possessed by the most gifted therapists and spiritual teachers. These talents trade upon access to the field of mind, which is also the basis for the congregational structures of a Gestalt Practice community. Even so, humans are prone to ignore these abilities in other life forms. For instance, the Earth is an immensely compassionate being that offers its resources for the support and awakening of other being, such as humans. Care and compassion can be shared in a relationship of support among all awakened beings.

Awareness supports formation of the human self. That self is the whole Gestalt of all the ways a person experiences themselves and others, including cognition, emotion, behavior and relationship. The continuity of selfhood is a characteristic pattern of the field, rather than something inherently inside the person.

Human psychological maladjustment exists when the organism deflects awareness of those experiences that consequently cannot be organized into a Gestalt of the self. However, when a person is able to accept all their experiences, they are able to form an integrated self. Maladjustment is the rigidity of an underdeveloped self, existing within an indistinct and truncated field of experience.

In Gestalt Practice, the operant paradigm is unbiased exploration of all experiences that might contribute to organization of the phenomenal field of self - whether or not those experiences are troublesome or pleasurable, boring or exciting. The objective of the method of Gestalt Practice is to facilitate the ability of a person to become an integrated self, embedded in their field.

Enhanced awareness is the primary tool of Gestalt Practice. Awareness is a form of experience that can be described as being in touch with one's existence - with one's body, with what one is feeling, thinking and imagining, and with what is actually happening in the surroundings - here and now. The subject of Gestalt Practice is the continuum of awareness - the ongoing process of Gestalt formation that brings the greatest need to the foreground, where it can be fully experienced and satisfied, so that it can then retreat into the background, leaving the foreground free for the next emergent need.

Effective human awareness is grounded in, and energized by, the dominant present human need of the organism. It involves not only self-knowledge, but also a direct knowledge of the current situation. Any denial of the situation and its demands, or of one's needs and the potential for satisfaction, is a disturbance of awareness. Meaningful awareness consists of a self in contact with the environment and "the other." Awareness is not an exclusive, inwardly focused introspection. Awareness is a field phenomenon that naturally includes the other.

The Gestalt concept of healthy functioning includes the operant factor of *creative adjustment*. This is the basic human process of equilibration between needs and resources that gives rise to a degree of organization and localized reduction of entropy. Health is characterized by the formation of "good Gestalts." This expression describes the organization of the perceptual field with clarity. A well-formed figure clearly stands out against a less distinct background. The relationship between that which stands out - the figure - and that which is context - the ground - is *meaning*. For a good Gestalt, the meaning is clear. The satisfaction of needs is a function of the emergent figure. Needs arise, are satisfied, and then fade into the background. In health, figure and ground shift smoothly, and awareness accurately represents the dominant need. So the concept of a good Gestalt provides a content-free existential definition of health.

Transformation of awareness can provide release from some of the more troublesome characteristics of human being. The Buddha said that the problem with existence was something he called *dukkha*, which has been translated from the Pali as suffering. In fact, if the Buddha had known about evolution he probably would have recognized competitive replication as the process underlying *dukkha*. Death provides a release from the evolutionary bondage of human existence. But human beings have an interesting capacity - they have the ability to develop their awareness in ways that allow for some measure of immediate transcendence.

Death is one method of transforming awareness. However, there are less cataclysmic ways of transforming human awareness. Of course, just as human character is fate, death is human destiny. That transformation is inevitable. And one might reasonably choose to do nothing more than await the inevitable with expectation and interest. But there are other modes of transforming awareness that humans can choose to engage in before their death. Working with awareness might be pursued as preparation for human death, with the objective of facilitating the final transition; or it might be pursued as a method for achieving a more healthy and expansive existence.

Death is usually misinterpreted as either extinction or reconstitution. Death is not the termination of awareness, but merely the dissolution of one particular process that organizes matter and energy. Because we experience human awareness as a fragile and fleeting process, we have developed a cult of fascination with what we imagine to be either its extinction, or complex forms of its resurrection. In fact, awareness is an endless characteristic of existence in which we mutually participate.

Death is not the end of awareness, but an awakening to what has been described, though not exhaustively, by those who are familiar with it, as a source-less luminosity or as transcendent awareness.

The human self is a persistent pattern
of mind. That pattern is a presence,
simultaneously embodied and transcendent,
in the field of mind.

When the process of embodiment breaks
down with death, the pattern of awareness
persists for a period in the transcendent
field of mind.

Eventually, following an ordinary process
of attenuation, the surviving pattern fades
into the background field of mind that is
analogous to (but not the same as) cosmic
background radiation.[3]

---

[3] Cosmic background radiation, which coincidently is a
remnant of photon decoupling, was discovered by accident
in 1965, and then interpreted as proof of current theories
about the origin of the Universe.

"Trust process, support process,
and get out of the way."
--Richard Price

www.ingramcontent.com/pod-product-compliance
Lightning Source LLC
Chambersburg PA
CBHW070345290526
45791CB00003B/1477